ADVENT
WITH THE
SAINTS

DAILY
REFLECTIONS

Greg Friedman,
O.F.M.

ST. ANTHONY MESSENGER PRESS
Cincinnati, Ohio

RESCRIPT

In accord with the Code of Canon Law, I hereby grant my permission to publish *Advent With the Saints: Daily Reflections*, by Greg Friedman, O.F.M.

Most Reverend Joseph R. Binzer
Vicar General
of the Archdiocese of Cincinnati
Cincinnati, Ohio
June 10, 2011

Cover and book design by Mark Sullivan
Cover image © Veer

LIBRARY OF CONGRESS CATALOGING-IN-PUBLICATION DATA
Friedman, Greg.
Advent with the saints : daily reflections / Greg Friedman.
p. cm.
ISBN 978-1-61636-132-7 (alk. paper)
1. Advent—Prayers and devotions. 2. Devotional calendars—
Catholic Church. 3. Catholic Church—Prayers and devotions. I.
Title.
BX2170.A4F75 2011
242'.332—dc23

2011017397

ISBN 978-1-61636-132-7

Published by St. Anthony Messenger Press
28 W. Liberty St.
Cincinnati, OH 45202

www.AmericanCatholic.org
www.SAMPBooks.org

Printed in the United States of America.
Printed on acid-free paper.

11 12 13 14 15   5 4 3 2 1

<h1 style="text-align:center">• • • | • • •
Contents</h1>

• • • | • • •

Introduction

In the *Fioretti*, the "Little Flowers" of St. Francis of Assisi, there's a strange story of how Francis sends his small group of brothers out into the world on mission. He tells them all to begin spinning, like tops. Obediently, they begin to turn around and around, until each collapses from dizziness. Francis then surveys them, lying on the ground, and tells them to go two by two in the direction in which they've fallen.

In choosing the saints for this book, I figuratively spun around several times, and found myself pointing in various directions. First, I thought of the meaning of the Advent season, a time of "joyful, expectant waiting," as described by my Franciscan confrere, liturgist Fr. Tom Richstatter, O.F.M. And so I thought of saints who waited patiently for some spiritual goal.

At the same time, I was guided in a different direction by the *Lectionary* for the weekdays of the Advent season. These rich, poetic selections—many from the Book of Isaiah—point to the ways in which God's promises will be fulfilled in Jesus. Following the homiletic practice of another Franciscan confrere, Fr. Jeff Scheeler, O.F.M., I looked for one simple idea or phrase that struck me in a particular day's readings. Then I went looking for a saint who matched it.

Another direction was offered by the saints who grace the calendar in the month of December, some of whom fit quite well with the spirit of the Scriptures at daily Mass.

The editors of this book also sent me spinning during the process, reminding me to keep diversity in my mix of saints—gender, time period, geography, and so forth. Where I've failed to do so in this Advent book, I hope to compensate in a companion volume for Lent.

To ward off dizziness through all of this, I grounded my selections in the key characters of the Christmas story—from both the Old and New Testaments. Were it up to me, I'd include all these holy men and women in *my* nativity scene, even unlikely visitors like Ruth and Isaiah—all three of him!

I dedicate this work to a beloved comrade-in-writing, Carol Luebering, whose presence across the office so many years ago taught a young writer and editor much about wisdom, warmth, and pastoral good sense. May her gentle smile now warm the halls of heaven!

First Week
of Advent

First Sunday of Advent

Isaiah: The Poet of Advent

YEAR A: ISAIAH 2:1–5; PSALM 122:1–2, 3–4, 4–5, 6–7, 8–9;
ROMANS 13:11–14; MATTHEW 24:37–44

YEAR B: ISAIAH 63:16B–17, 19B; 64:2–7; PSALM 80:2–3, 15–16, 18–19 (4);
1 CORINTHIANS 1:3–9; MARK 13:33–37

YEAR C: JEREMIAH 33:14–16; PSALM 25:4–5, 8–9, 10, 14 (1B); 1
THESSALONIANS 3:12—4:2; LUKE 21:25–28, 34–36

Each Christmas I try to write a poem to include in my Christmas card—poetry seems fitting for the dark winter days before Christmas. The liturgy opts for poetry as well, much of it to be found in our Advent readings from the book of Isaiah. Some call it the "Fifth Gospel," since the evangelists quote from Isaiah so extensively.

Some Bible scholars believe the book is actually the work of three different prophetic voices, over a period stretching from the eighth to the sixth century before Christ. Another theory sees a more unified work, centered on chapters 40—55, dating from the sixth century BC, when Israel was in exile in Babylon. The hope for the restoration of God's people is focused in these chapters; and some suggest that the rest of the book was then collected from earlier traditions attributed to the original Isaiah.

Theories aside, our Advent selections from Isaiah are among the most beautiful in the Bible, touching upon poetic imagery of deserts blooming, mountains lowering, and valleys filling up to provide a way for the coming of the Lord. Here we find words of comfort and hope for all times, centering on the coming of the Messiah, who is named "Emmanuel," "God with us."

May we allow the poetry of Isaiah to color our Advent waiting!

Today's Action
Use a Bible or worship aid from your parish to find your favorite Advent passage from Isaiah. Then read aloud the passage to hear its poetry.

Prayer
God of our poetry, write new lines in our lives this season. May our hearts resound with the prophets' promises, fulfilled in Emmanuel, God-with-us, Jesus our Lord. Amen.

• • • | • • •

Monday of the First Week of Advent

St. Frances Xavier Cabrini: A Saint for Immigrants

Isaiah 2:1–5 (alternate for Year A, Isaiah 4:2–6);
Psalm 122:1–2, 3–4, (4–5, 6–7) 8–9; Matthew 8:5–11

Much of the Catholic Church in the United States has grown through the faith of thousands of immigrants who came here over two centuries. Many of them arrived in the second half of the nineteenth and the first part of the twentieth century.

Among them was Mother Frances Xavier Cabrini, who came from Italy at the direction of Pope Leo XIII. Although she had wished to become a missionary to China, she readily embraced the call to serve her fellow immigrants, beginning in New York City. Over thirty-five years, she oversaw the establishment of sixty-seven institutions to care for those who were poor, outcast, sick, orphaned, or in need of education.

Mother Cabrini bore many of the same hardships as her fellow immigrants. Like many of them, she embraced her new homeland and became a citizen—and its first canonized saint.

In today's Scripture Isaiah celebrates the nations coming to Jerusalem, while Jesus commends the faith of a foreigner, a Roman centurion.

May we be as welcoming as our God to those who are strangers or in need during this holy season—and beyond.

Today's Action
Take time to study the statements the U.S. bishops have made on immigration, which can be found at: http://www.justiceforimmigrants.org/index.shtml.

Prayer
God of immigrants, walk with all those who leave their home to find freedom and security. Help us form a wise community of justice to welcome your Son's healing word. Amen.

Tuesday of the First Week of Advent

Bl. Adolph Kolping (December 4): Preserving the Dignity of Workers and Family

Isaiah 11:1–10; Psalm 72:1, 7–8, 12–13, 17; Luke 10:21–24

My hometown of Cincinnati has a German flavor, thanks to thousands of immigrants who arrived in the nineteenth century. Their homeland was undergoing many changes as factories and industry grew. The dignity of workers and the sanctity of family were threatened. In the late 1840s, a German priest, Father Adolph Kolping, began a society that soon spread around the world and still flourishes today, with many thousands of members.

The "Kolping Society," as it is popularly known, seeks to emphasize the dignity of human work and support family life. It envisions a world based on God's heavenly reign, described in today's first reading.

In Isaiah's beautiful description of God's dream for the world, God's sevenfold gifts are given to the Messiah. We see these traits of wisdom, understanding, counsel, strength, knowledge, wonder, and awe as the "Gifts of the Holy Spirit," present in Jesus. These gifts are promised to us by Christ; we celebrate the gifts of the Spirit in the sacraments. In today's Gospel we are invited to share the life he has with the Father and to be part of their intimate relationship.

Bl. Adolph Kolping sought to promote the benefits of that life-giving relationship in human society, where God's dream of a peaceful, harmonious world, can come true.

Today's Action

Check online to learn more about the goals of Kolping International and to see if there is a chapter near you: http://www.kolping.net/en/international.

Prayer

God of family and hearth, teach us how to embody your dream for the world. May our homes and families be gardens of peace, an echo of the promise of your heavenly reign. Amen.

· · · | · · ·

Wednesday of the First Week of Advent

St. Vincent de Paul and Bl. Frederic Ozanam: Caring for the Poor

Isaiah 25:6–10; Psalm 23:1–3, 3–4, 5, 6; Matthew 15:29–37

My inner-city parish is blessed to host a soup kitchen, supported by generous volunteers and benefactors. They welcome people who are homeless or lack the means to set their own table. Our soup kitchen guests are often quick to acknowledge God as the source of the goodness they experience. They remind me how frequently I forget to be grateful. Perhaps a little more hunger in my life would help my awareness!

Meals are a familiar metaphor for God's goodness in the Scriptures. Today we have two biblical references: a heavenly banquet thrown by God and Jesus' miraculous feeding of the crowds.

Saints throughout history have been moved to help the work of God's reign by feeding and caring for the poor. St. Vincent de Paul inspired men and women in the seventeenth century to devote their lives to the service of those on the margins of society. Almost two centuries later, Bl. Frederic Ozanam created a parish-based approach to helping the poor and named it after Vincent de Paul. The St. Vincent de Paul society flourishes to this day.

Christmastime is marked by extra efforts at generosity toward the poor, and rightly so, since Jesus was born in a poor setting, and his birth was heralded by both poor shepherds and wise men bringing gifts.

May our Christmas giving include God's poor—and move us all to greater gratitude!

Today's Action

Discover a way to practice some "alternative giving" that benefits others in need.

Prayer

God of the poor, we hear of your care through the ages. You welcome all to your heavenly banquet. Your Son offers us the Bread of eternal life. May we receive it with gratitude and pledge our service to others. Amen.

• • • | • • •

Thursday of the First Week of Advent

St. Peter: Building the Church on "Rocky Johnson"

ISAIAH 26:1–6; PSALM 118:1, 8–9, 19–21, 25–27A; MATTHEW 7:21, 24–27

One of my seminary professors once startled us in class by referring to St. Peter as "Rocky Johnson." It's true! The man Jesus picked as chief apostle was "Simon, son of John," given the nickname *Cephas*, meaning "Rock," by Jesus.

Our Scriptures today play with the same imagery: the "Rock" who is our God. In relationship with God, we find the same security the ancients found of living in a well-fortified city. The prophet Isaiah asks us to put an even deeper trust in God.

Jesus takes the image and applies it to the faithful disciple who hears Jesus' words and acts on them, comparing such a follower to a man who wisely built his house on rock.

No wonder, then, that Jesus saw qualities in Peter that prompted the nickname "Rocky." We're left to speculate what physical and emotional traits might have prompted the title. The Gospel stories do give us clues in a number of tantalizing moments when Peter interacted with Jesus. He accepted Peter's profession of faith, and challenged him to follow on the way of the cross. Jesus never lost faith in Peter, despite Peter's human weaknesses.

What traits does Jesus see in you and me? What "grounds" our relationship with Christ?

Today's Action
Reflect on someone who has followed Jesus well and how that person can inspire you in your own relationship to Christ.

Prayer
God, who is our rock and our foundation, root us in you. May the storms of life not shake our inmost calm, which comes through the life and peace of your Son, Jesus. Amen.

Friday of the First Week of Advent

St. Lucy (December 13): Seeking Christ Our Light
ISAIAH 29:17–24; PSALM 27:1, 4, 13–14; MATTHEW 9:27–31

As I grow older, I value my eyesight more and more. Some years ago, I underwent cataract surgery on both eyes. The experience was sobering. As the surgeon slipped my natural lens out and I was momentarily blinded, I realized just what my sight meant to me.

No wonder the restoration of sight is an important biblical metaphor. Isaiah uses it as a sign of God's transformation of the world. In Matthew's Gospel it is a sign of the reign of God.

We must be careful in our use of this metaphor. Those sightless from birth or through illness or injury are nevertheless full persons. But both Scripture and tradition use sight as a metaphor, as we do in common speech, when we say, "I see," to indicate our understanding.

Fourth-century martyr St. Lucy is honored by a feast in the midst of the Advent season. Little is known about her life, except that she died a martyr's death after a would-be suitor denounced her as a Christian. She is depicted in art holding her eyes on a plate, and so legends developed that her eyes were gouged out by her torturers. Perhaps her name, which means "light," helped those stories to grow, until Lucy became, in the tradition of the church, the patron of those who are blind.

In the dark days of winter, let us seek Christ, that we may truly see ourselves in his Light.

Today's Action
Light the first Advent wreath candle today and spend some time in prayer.

Prayer
God who enlightens the world through the coming of your Son, fill our lives with light in these winter days. Help us carry the light into others' darkness. Amen.

Saturday of the First Week of Advent

St. Francis Xavier (December 3): A Church in Mission

Isaiah 30:19–21, 23–26; Psalm 147:1–2, 3–4, 5–6;
Matthew 9:35—10:1, 6–8

Mission is the theme in today's Gospel, as Jesus tours the towns and villages, proclaiming God's heavenly reign. There, he recognizes how great the need was among the people. So he sends out his twelve disciples and empowers them to drive out demons, cure sickness, and announce the reign of God.

Generations of Christians have been moved by that same missionary impulse. St. Francis Xavier, in the sixteenth century, heard the gospel challenge from his friend, Ignatius of Loyola. Francis was resistant at first, but the persistent Ignatius finally prevailed, and Francis joined his fledgling "Society of Jesus" in 1534.

Francis embarked on a missionary journey after his ordination in 1537. It took him to the East Indies, where he preached to Indians, Malayans, and the Japanese. He lived with the poor, embracing their lot. His letters attest to his joy in the midst of hardship. Francis spent ten years in mission work, until death intervened before he could realize his dream of preaching in China.

Francis Xavier lived out the command of Jesus in today's Advent Gospel: "The gift you have received, give as a gift."

Today's Action
Pray today for the missionaries from your home diocese who are working in various parts of the world.

Prayer
God, who sends us on mission, help us to be Good News for all we meet. In words or in actions, may all we do be signs of your love. Amen.

Second Week
of Advent

· · · | · · ·

Second Sunday of Advent

St. John the Baptist: Prepare the Way

YEAR A: ISAIAH 11:1–10; PSALM 72:1–2, 7–8, 12–13, 17 (SEE 7);
ROMANS 15:4–9; MATTHEW 2:1–2
YEAR B: ISAIAH 40:1–5, 9–11; PSALM 85:9–10, 11–12, 13–14 (8);
2 PETER 3:8–14; MARK 1:1–8
YEAR C: BARUCH 5:1–9; PSALM 126:1–2, 2–3, 4–5, 6 (3);
PHILIPPIANS 1:4–6, 8–11; LUKE 3:1–6

John the Baptist takes center stage in the Gospels in all three *Lectionary* cycles on the Second and Third Sundays of Advent. He strides dramatically onto the scene, preaching in the desert and calling people to baptism.

His camel's hair clothing and diet of locusts and honey make him what my friend, religious writer Carol Luebering, called "the kind of person who causes parents to draw their children closer as he passes… the prototype of a thousand cartoons, an incongruous figure proclaiming the immanence of the day of judgment." In Franco Zeffirelli's *Jesus of Nazareth*, actor Michael York gives a classic portrayal of John and his preaching.

John's message is indeed one of challenge. He makes it clear that to prepare for the coming of the promised Messiah, we must repent and make his paths straight. Here he echoes his Old Testament counterpart, and fellow Advent prophet, Isaiah.

John appears on the Biblical stage for only a short time. He's eager to step aside and make way for Christ. But even Our Lord takes a moment in Matthew 11 (Thursday of the Second Week of Advent) to acknowledge John's place in the story of salvation. May we likewise find a place for the message of repentance as we make ready for Christmas.

Today's Action
As part of your Advent preparation for Christmas, pick up your Bible and read how each of the four Gospels depicts John the Baptist.

Prayer
God, who comes into our world in Jesus, help us build roadways of peace into the lives which intersect with ours. May we never be obstacles in others' paths. Amen.

・ ・ ・ | ・ ・ ・

Monday of the Second Week of Advent

St. Nicholas (December 6): Unexpected and Surprising Gifts

ISAIAH 35:1–10; PSALM 85:9–10, 11–12, 13–14; LUKE 5:17–26

It's well known that St. Nicholas, a sixth-century bishop, is behind our use of the secular "icon" of Christmas, Santa Claus. The legends of Nicholas involve his generosity to those in need. The most famous story involves how he anonymously tossed a bag of money through a window to provide the dowry of a young woman who would otherwise be forced into an unpleasant marriage. The details of Nicholas's life are few; but legends often have a kernel of truth, and if so, he forms a worthy basis for reflection during this season of preparation for Christmas.

Jesus' earthly ministry was full of unexpected and surprising gifts. In today's Gospel he offers the gift of healing and forgiveness to a man who comes, not through the window, but through the roof, to encounter Jesus.

The dramatic scene of a paralyzed figured being lowered into a dim and dusty circle of people, to the feet of

Jesus, parallels the dramatic "breaking in" of God's reign. The prophet Isaiah in today's First Reading points to such dramatic transformations.

Advent is a time to expect God's intervention in our lives. It may be dramatic, or—more typically—quiet and perhaps not immediately evident. God may even use a bit of stealth, as the legendary Nicholas did, to gift us. May we keep the windows of our heart open!

Today's Action
Become a "secret St. Nicholas" for someone with an anonymous gift.

Prayer
God of surprises, startle us today with your unexpected gifts of love. May we see them in familiar faces and places and respond in kind! Amen.

• • • | • • •

Tuesday of the Second Week of Advent

St. Monica: Our Expectant Waiting

ISAIAH 40:1–11; PSALM 96:1–2, 3, 10, 11–12, 13; MATTHEW 18:12–14

Advent is a season of waiting. The Scriptures fill us with hope, based on the promises of God. Many of these promises, especially in the Advent readings from Isaiah, describe healing, comfort, a return to God.

Today's first reading urges the prophet to comfort God's people, to tell them their suffering is at an end. They are to make ready to welcome God's coming in both power and gentleness.

One saint who models both an expectant waiting and the strength and gentleness of a mother is St. Monica. This fourth-century Christian woman was married to a pagan with a fierce temper and immoral ways. His household included a bad-tempered mother-in-law.

Monica is best known for her long years of prayer, waiting for the conversion of her son, Augustine. Her prayers were answered for her son, as well as for her husband and mother-in-law!

Augustine's conversion took the longest—thirty-three years. He became a Christian, a bishop, and one of the greatest Christian teachers of all time.

Monica's perseverance and example of faith-filled waiting saw her lifelong dream fulfilled. Like the shepherd in today's Gospel who searches for the one lost sheep out of a hundred, Monica reminds us of how much our God seeks us out and longs for our return.

Today's Action
Thank God for someone who has prayed for you in your times of need.

Prayer
God of our expectant waiting, hear the longing in our hearts. Where we are tempted to give up hope, refresh us with your presence and peace. Amen.

Wednesday of the Second Week of Advent

St. John of the Cross (December 14):
Self–Denial, the Cross, and Discipleship

Isaiah 40:25–31; Psalm 103:1–2, 3–4, 8, 10; Matthew 11:28–30

It may seem strange to think of the cross during a season that prepares us for Christmas. In today's Gospel, however, Jesus invites us to take his yoke upon our shoulders. As his disciples we are invited to embrace the cross, and so find life in losing it.

St. John of the Cross is a saint who lived the cross almost literally. A sixteenth-century Spanish priest who worked with St. Teresa of Avila to reform their Carmelite Order, John met resistance and persecution and spent many months in the darkness of a prison cell.

His experience opened him to a profound understanding of the darkness of the soul, the power of mortification, and the challenges of embracing the cross.

He articulated his spiritual journey in works such as his *Ascent to Mt. Carmel.* As spiritual director and theologian (he was later named a doctor of the church), John—in his mystical prose and poetry—teaches an important dimension of Christian life.

While the rigors of John's life may not be our path, all of us can benefit from learning how God met him in the darkness of his soul, in times of suffering and loss, and in the denial of self, which Jesus tells us is absolutely essential if we are to be his disciples.

Today's Action
Examine your life in the light of the cross and the darkness of your soul.

Prayer
God who calls us to the cross, give us strength to carry our own cross. May we first recognize it and then shoulder it with your help, denying self and finding only you. Amen.

Thursday of the Second Week of Advent

Our Lady of Guadalupe (December 12) and St. Juan Diego (December 9): The Wasteland Blooms

Isaiah 41:13–20; Psalm 145:1, 9, 10–11, 12–13; Matthew 11:11–15

A desert becomes a marshland, and a wasteland flourishes with cypress and pine trees. A thirsty people find refreshment there. So Isaiah today describes God's care for Israel.

Roses bloom in the winter and a miraculous image of a young Native American woman garbed as an Aztec princess appears on the cloak of a poor man in Mexico in 1531. Through it, the peoples of the Americas come to honor Mary in a new devotion that has flourished for almost five hundred years.

Anyone who has lived or worked in Latin America or in the United States among Hispanic Catholics knows the warmth of their love and affection for Our Lady of Guadalupe. Pilgrims flock to the great church built on the site where Juan Diego, a Native American convert, whose Indian name was Cuauhtlatohuac, saw the vision of the young woman on Tepeyac hill near Mexico City and carried her request to build a church to the local bishop.

The bishop's demand for a sign led to the miracle of the roses that fell from Juan Diego's *tilma*, which revealed the image of the woman in the fabric. Appearing there as she does, in the image of the native Aztec people, reinforces our faith in the fundamental truth of God enfleshed in humanity—the truth we will celebrate at Christmas.

Today's Action
Buy a small plant for your home as a symbol of hope in God's promises.

Prayer
God the gardener, plant in us a green oasis like Eden, or the prophet's promised place of refreshment. May we find such a place at Eucharist and in the quiet of our prayer. Amen.

Friday of the Second Week of Advent

St. Angela Merici: God, Our Teacher

Isaiah 48:17–19; Psalm 1:1–2, 3, 4, 6; Matthew 11:16–19

Many Catholics of my generation and older have been influenced by women religious who educated us as young Catholics. In my life, it was the Ursuline Sisters, founded in the early sixteenth century by Angela Merici. The Ursulines were the first Catholic women's congregation devoted to teaching.

Angela joined the lay Franciscan movement while still a young woman. She was attracted to a life of simplicity, and moved to work with poor children as a teacher. She was gifted with gifts of leadership that drew others to her.

She gathered others around her who shared her vision. But it was not until her late fifties that her "Company of St. Ursula" took shape. Their goal was to reinvigorate Christian life by training women for marriage and family life.

A good teacher, in a real sense, is doing the work of God. In today's passage from Isaiah, God claims the role of teacher, leading us and offering the commandments as the way to life. Let us be grateful for Angela, and those who came after her, who taught us in the faith, and in doing so, imitated our God.

Today's Action
Say a prayer of thanks for those who formed your faith and for any special teachers who have graced your life.

Prayer
God our teacher, instill in us lessons of charity. Let the great teachers of old live in our words and deeds today, and may the teachings of your Son shine through all we are. Amen.

Saturday of the Second Week of Advent

Elijah: Prophet of the End Times

SIRACH 48:1–4, 9–11; PSALM 80:2–3, 15–16, 18–19; MATTHEW 17:10–13

One of the religious cable channels regularly runs old, and usually forgettable, movies about biblical heroes. Somewhere in that collection is probably one about the prophet Elijah made in the 1950s, but now unavailable. The prophet deserves better!

He doesn't rate a book of his own in the Hebrew Scriptures, but his exploits span the first and second books of Kings. There, he plays a key role in the salvation story.

Elijah fights to keep the traditional faith in God pure amidst attacks from worshipers of Baal. A scene worthy of Hollywood has him summon fire from heaven to consume an offering—and conveniently, the prophets of Baal! He's also featured in a number of miracle stories.

But of interest to us today are two other parts of his story: Elijah is depicted leaving the earth in a fiery chariot, implying that he did not die, and will return again.

Also, Elijah proclaims the "day of the Lord," the end-times' fulfillment of God's plan.

The New Testament—in fact, Jesus himself—connects Elijah's return with John the Baptist. In today's Gospel Jesus describes John's role, and hints at his own passion and death—a sober reminder of the shadow of the cross that looms over the crib.

Today's Action
Take time to read some of the Elijah stories in 1 and 2 Kings.

Prayer
God of the prophets, fire us with zeal for all that is right and just. Keep our hearts single-minded and help us in turn to speak your truths to others. Amen.

Third Week
of Advent

· · · | · · ·

Third Sunday of Advent
Mary: Faithful Disciple
YEAR A: ISAIAH 35:1–6A, 10; PSALM 146:6–7, 8–9, 9–10
(SEE ISAIAH 35:4); JAMES 5:7–10; MATTHEW 11:2–11
YEAR B: ISAIAH 61:1–2A, 10–11; LUKE 1:46–48, 49–50, 53–54
(ISAIAH 61:10B); 1 THESSALONIANS 5:16–24; JOHN 1:6–8, 19–28
YEAR C: ZEPHANIAH 3:14–18A; PSALM 12:2–3, 4, 5–6 (6);
PHILIPPIANS 4:4–7; LUKE 3:10–18

In our nativity scenes, the image of the Blessed Mother draws our line of sight from her eyes to the Infant Jesus. And that is as it should be.

Mary captures our hearts in the Christmas story. Her story evokes the dilemma of a young unwed mother, the challenge of a pregnancy in difficult times, the heartbreak of a son killed in the course of his mission.

However, the Gospel of Luke, our chief source for the story of the Blessed Mother, would have us focus on a deeper dimension. Scripture scholar Fr. Raymond Brown links the Mary whom we see in the infancy stories with her portrayal later in the Gospel.

As the Christmas story concludes, we hear that Mary "treasured all these things in her heart." This phrase connects us to a scene in Luke 8, where Mary and other family members come to where Jesus is preaching. Jesus proclaims, "My mother and my brothers are those who hear the word of God and act on it."

This is the standard for discipleship: to hear the word and put it into action. From the Annunciation, through Jesus' birth and beyond, Mary is the model of the faithful disciple, drawing us close to Jesus.

Today's Action
Meditate on the figure of Mary in the nativity scene in the light of what it means to be a disciple.

Prayer
Faithful God, teach us how to hear your word and live it out, as Mary did. May she draw us closer to your Son, whom she bore into our world. Amen.

· · · | · · ·

Monday of the Third Week of Advent

St. Athanasius: Witnessing to the Incarnation

Readings used if today's date is not December 17 or 18:
Numbers 24:2–7, 15–17; Psalm 25:4–5, 6–7, 8–9; Matthew 21:23–27

The incarnation is at the heart of our faith, and what we celebrate in this season. Over the course of Christian history, it fell to a number of saints to help establish the truth of God-become-human. That effort was often a bitter struggle, resulting in great hardships.

In the fourth century, the Arian heresy tore the young church apart, as the teaching of the priest Arius denied the divinity of Christ. Thousands followed Arius, including many bishops.

Standing against Arianism was Athanasius, first as a deacon at the Council of Nicea, and later as bishop of Alexandria. The Creed we pray today bears, in part, the stamp of the work of Athanasius and his colleagues. In his defense of Christ's divinity, Athanasius faced great opposition and suffered exile five times.

In today's Gospel Jesus' authority is called into question by the chief priests and scribes as he teaches in the temple. They are not ready to accept his divine mandate. He silences his opponents with a clever argument.

Athanasius witnesses to Christ by his preaching, writing, and silent suffering in exile. We, too, can find a variety of opportunities to profess our faith in Jesus.

Today's Action
Consider what form your witness to Christ might take.

Prayer
God who inspires, stand behind our witness in the world. May our lives lead others to the mystery of your love, made visible in Jesus your Son. Amen.

Tuesday of the Third Week of Advent

St. Josephine Bakhita: God Chooses a Remnant

Readings used if today's date is not December 17 or 18:
Zephaniah 3:1–2, 9–13; Psalm 34:2–3, 6–7, 17–18, 19, 23;
Matthew 21:28–32

The bitter history of slavery in the United States has been called by one historian "the original sin" of our country. We still feel its effects today in our society.

The sin of slavery has indeed marked many parts of the world. In the late nineteenth century a seven-year-old African girl was kidnapped and sold into slavery. Her name was Bakhita, meaning "fortunate."

She eventually came into the possession of an Italian family in Africa and was babysitter for the daughter of the family. The daughter's conversion moved Bakhita to faith in Jesus, and she was baptized Josephine in 1890.

But slavery's grip was strong. When the Italian family who claimed her wanted to return to Italy, Josephine refused. A court battle followed. The patriarch of Venice, and the Canossian sisters, whom Josephine had met on a visit there while caring for her Italian charge, took Josephine's case. The court ruled in her favor, since Italy had banned slavery some years earlier.

As a free woman, Josephine joined the Canossian sisters and was professed as a religious. She served the community and the poor, and was widely beloved, until her death in 1947.

Today's reading from the prophet Zephaniah proclaims that God will uphold a remnant of the people, from among the poor and lowly. Josephine would have understood!

Today's Action

Pray today for women and girls throughout the world victimized by violence and trafficking.

Prayer

God who chooses a remnant of Israel, choose us as well when we feel lost and alone. Stand with those whom our world shuts out or abuses. Be their strength always. Amen.

Wednesday of the Third Week of Advent

St. Katharine Drexel: Signs of God's Reign

READINGS USED IF TODAY'S DATE IS NOT DECEMBER 17 OR 18:
ISAIAH 45:6–8, 18, 21–25; PSALM 85:9–10, 11–12, 13–14; LUKE 7:18–23

In today's Gospel Jesus sends a report to John the Baptist, who is in prison. John's disciples are to take back word of what Jesus is doing: curing the sick and physically disabled, raising the dead, and preaching good news to the poor. Indeed, John's hopes in God's promises to Israel, the advent of the reign of God, had been fulfilled in Jesus.

Such a report might have been given about Katharine Drexel's nearly century-long life. Born in the mid-nineteenth century to great wealth and social status, she was profoundly transformed by the experience of nursing a terminally ill family member. She was moved to put her share of the family's great wealth to use. Pope Leo XIII, who also was responsible for sending Italian Frances Cabrini to do missionary work in America, told Katharine to pursue a similar vocation.

The result: a long history of good works by Katharine and the religious congregation she founded, the Sisters of the Blessed Sacrament. They specialized in teaching and assisting the lives not only of Native Americans, but African Americans as well.

Truly, the record of Mother Katharine's life is part of how Jesus has brought God's reign into reality in our world, with works of healing, teaching and proclaiming Good News.

Today's Action

Become a missionary in your own community by some witness or work of charity.

Prayer

God of both rich and poor, give to all, in every station of life, the impulse to do your will. When we are gifted with much, make us generous. When we receive from others, make us grateful. Amen.

Thursday of the Third Week of Advent

St. Elizabeth Ann Seton: Woman of Tenderness and Strength

READINGS USED IF TODAY'S DATE IS NOT DECEMBER 17 OR 18:
ISAIAH 54:1–10; PSALM 30:2, 4, 5–6, 11–12, 13; LUKE 7:24–30

The prophets often use the metaphor of interrupted marriage to describe the relationship between God and Israel—a metaphor entwined with cultural values distant from our own. Israel is sometimes compared to the wife who has been unfaithful. God is the spouse who abandons. The metaphors can be problematic for us, in a way they were not for the original audience.

In today's first reading Isaiah uses the metaphor, in a passage describing how God restores the relationship with Israel, described in turn as a deserted wife, a widow, and then "forsaken and grieved in spirit."

Finding a saint to delicately balance against the ancient metaphor is a challenge. One who endured young widowhood, misunderstanding, and poverty, and found sainthood in service is Elizabeth Ann Seton, first American-born citizen to be canonized.

Mother Seton found consolation and conversion in the Catholic faith after her husband's death. Many obstacles remained, as she raised five children while attempting to start a school in the fledgling United States. She went on to found the Sisters of Charity, first women's religious congregation in America, and give her country its first parish school and Catholic orphanage. She remains a powerful example for her religious family, which still flourishes today, and embodies a tenderness and strength that might resonate with old Isaiah as well!

Today's Action
Call a widow or widower in your parish or neighborhood and offer your friendship.

Prayer
God of the forsaken, be with us when we feel abandoned. Be the silent strength in our depths, to sustain us, and lead us to life. Amen.

Friday of the Third Week of Advent

Bl. John XXIII: Good Pope John

READINGS USED IF TODAY'S DATE IS NOT DECEMBER 17 OR 18:
ISAIAH 56:1–3, 6–8; PSALM 67:2–3, 5, 7–8; JOHN 5:33–36

Outside a Franciscan church in Istanbul stands a bronze statue of Pope John XXIII. It is a testimony to his diplomatic service during World War II, when as Archbishop Angelo Roncalli, he helped save some twenty-four thousand Jews from Nazi clutches. He is still remembered fondly among the Turkish people of all faiths.

Today's First Reading from Isaiah declares, "Let not the foreigner say, when he would join himself to the Lord, 'The Lord will surely exclude me from his people.'" To an Israel that regarded foreigners as unclean, this was a prophetic challenge. In our time, that challenge is retranslated into how the church approaches other religions.

Angelo Roncalli brought an ecumenical vision to the papacy. He called the Second Vatican Council and opened the church to the world in dialogue. The council welcomed observers from other faiths and gave the church a social justice agenda, echoed by the pope in his encyclical "Peace on Earth."

In today's Gospel Jesus praises John the Baptist as a messenger of God's reign. In our day, "Good Pope John" carried the message of the Good News to the world with graciousness and humor. May we imitate him as we encounter others in the name of Christ.

Today's Action
Plan in the new year to visit a local mosque or church of another faith tradition.

Prayer
God who welcomes all, let us discover your Spirit at work in everyone of good will. Help us to join in dialogue with all who seek peace on earth. Amen.

Note: Eight days before Christmas, the Lectionary provides a separate cycle of readings for December 17–22.

Fourth Week
of Advent

Fourth Sunday of Advent

St. Joseph: Silent in His Fidelity

YEAR A: ISAIAH 7:10–14; PSALM 24:1–2, 3–4, 5–6 (7C, 10B);
ROMANS 1:1–7; MATTHEW 1:18–24
YEAR B: 2 SAMUEL 7:1–5, 8B–12, 14A, 16; PSALM 89:2–3, 4–5, 27, 29 (2A);
ROMANS 16:25–27; LUKE 1:26–38
YEAR C: MICAH 5:1–4A; PSALM 80:2–3, 15–16, 18–19 (4);
HEBREWS 10:5–10; LUKE 1:39–45

Joseph is the silent figure in the Christmas stories. We never hear him speak; his annunciation—in Matthew's Gospel—narrates Joseph's story without giving us any of his words. But his actions speak loudly!

Matthew's goal is to show us Joseph as part of the fulfillment of God's promises in the Hebrew Scriptures. Matthew's complex genealogy ends with Joseph, linking Jesus with King David.

Where Luke features Mary as the star of his infancy story, Matthew's hero is Joseph, portrayed as a truly "just man," the ideal observer of the Law. His decision to divorce Mary quietly is a compassionate approach to the Law, even *before* he knows her pregnancy is miraculous.

Like his Old Testament namesake, Joseph is a dreamer, and his dreams reveal God's plans for the Messiah. When he learns the truth of Mary's pregnancy in a dream, he acts to fulfill his role in God's plan. When he learns in a dream of the danger to the child, he takes Jesus and Mary to Egypt—another reference to the story of salvation.

In each instance, Joseph acts with wisdom and faithfulness to carry out God's plan. May our actions speak loudly of our faithfulness to God!

Today's Action
Use silence today as part of your response to God.

Prayer
God of our silences, speak in the depths of our heart. Gift us to recognize your voice beyond words. Above all, may we be patient enough to wait for your voice. Amen.

· · · | · · ·

December 17

Ruth: A Family Record of Fidelity

<small>Genesis 49:2, 8–10; Psalm 72:3–4, 7–8, 17; Matthew 1:1–17</small>

The American Scripture scholar Fr. Raymond Brown once commented that the genealogy in Matthew's Gospel is one of the least-appreciated parts of the Bible. For many a preacher and congregation this list of names and "begats" elicits groans.

Fr. Brown, on the other hand, wanted to see it receive more attention. This family record of Jesus deserves our focus—if only for the assembly of interesting, and controversial, biblical characters. Essential to the list are five women whose stories are touched by unique circumstances.

One of these is Ruth, a pagan woman, who was widowed, along with her sister and her Hebrew mother-in-law, Naomi. When Naomi urges her daughters-in-law to go and seek new husbands among their own people, Ruth refuses. She chooses to accompany Naomi back to the land of Israel. There, she becomes part of the story of our salvation, as the woman who will be the grandmother of King David and an ancestor of Jesus.

Ruth's story is one of the most touching in all of Scripture. She is a model of fidelity and of enduring relationships that mark the story of God's relationship with us. In a season when family ties often are a main focus, let's remember Ruth and how she teaches us about our identity as human and divine families.

Today's Action
Take time to read and study Matthew 1:1–17, the genealogy of Jesus.

Prayer
God of our history, we thank you for those who bequeathed their faith to us, especially in the bonds of family. May we accept the gift given to us and share it with the next generation. Amen.

· · · | · · ·

King David: Royal Forgiveness

Jeremiah 23:5–8; Psalm 72:1, 12–13, 18–19; Matthew 1:18–24

I must confess in my years of studying the Bible, I have not been a big fan of King David. He seems to have a pampered relationship with God, doing whatever he wants without the consequences others suffer. David commits adultery and has the woman's husband murdered. He disobeys God's command not to take a census, and as a result the people—not the king—bear the brunt of the punishment. David's later life is marked by dissolute living.

True, he suffers the loss of his beloved Absalom, son of the adulterous relationship with Bathsheba—and David grieves. But in much of the story David bounces back again and again. God keeps forgiving him.

In recent years, however, my attitude has changed. I've begun to realize how my harsh verdict on David is the way *I* would treat him. I judge others and myself the same way. So often, I do not imitate God's forgiveness, even though like David, I have been forgiven and offered other chances—many, many times.

The biblical stories of Advent present Jesus as the Son of David. Matthew's story of Joseph's dream in today's Gospel helps reinforce that connection. Unlike his ancestor, Jesus is sinless. He embodies the forgiveness of God that was lavished on King David, and he brings that same forgiveness to us.

Today's Action

Spend a few moments counting—not merely your blessings—but the times you've been forgiven by God.

Prayer

God of forgiveness, lavish on us the love you showed your servant David. Move us to admit, as he did, our sinfulness, and open us to your mercy. Amen.

December 19

Zechariah: Standing on the Shoulders of Giants

JUDGES 13:2–7, 24–25; PSALM 71:3–4, 5–6, 16–17; LUKE 1:5–25

In the final days of Advent, the Lectionary unrolls the tapestry of Luke's infancy story in our weekday Gospels. These stories are charming, but behind them is a carefully woven structure.

Luke wants to convey how the Good News fulfilled all of God's promises throughout salvation history. And so, Luke deliberately echoes figures from Israel's history.

Today's Gospel portrays the Annunciation to Zechariah. He is a priest, fulfilling his liturgical duties in the temple, when he is visited by the angelic messenger Gabriel. The message: Zechariah and his wife Elizabeth, both advanced in age, will welcome a child, who will do his part in God's plan.

Luke has in mind not one, but two Old Testament couples, both elderly, both childless, and both destined to bear sons who will impact salvation history. He is thinking Abraham and Sarah in the Genesis story, and Elkanah and his wife, Hannah, parents of the prophet Samuel.

Luke even puts in Zechariah's mouth a quotation from Abraham, "How am I to know this?" expressing his disbelief at how God's plan will unfold.

Let's not be too negative about Zechariah's response. He's filling some pretty big sandals in the story. But that is how God works, through ordinary people taking part in an extraordinary story.

Today's Action
Reflect on your own family history, and the role of your ancestors in the gift of your faith.

Prayer
God of promises fulfilled, we delight in the stories of faith we share in this holy season. Let them inspire us anew to rejoice in your fidelity. Amen.

December 20

Gabriel: A Message of Fulfilled Promises

ISAIAH 7:10–14; PSALM 24:1–2, 3–4, 5–6; LUKE 1:26–38

Our focus in the Annunciation story is rightly on Mary and her "yes" to God's plan of salvation. But let's turn our attention for a moment on the messenger. Surely Mary would not mind!

The archangel Gabriel delivers two messages in Luke's story: one to Zechariah and one to Mary. Both concern a miraculous birth that fulfills God's plan.

These are not the first appearances of Gabriel in the Scriptures. In the book of Daniel, which scholars believe is perhaps the last book of the Hebrew Scriptures, Gabriel appears to the book's hero in dramatic visions. Daniel is awestruck and cannot speak, much like Zechariah when Gabriel appears to him in the temple.

Gabriel tells Daniel that, "Everlasting justice will be introduced, vision and prophecy ratified, and a most holy will be anointed." Scholars point out that Luke wants us to hear echoes of the Old Testament in his stories, where God's plan for salvation unfolds in the dramatic announcements and births of John the Baptist and Jesus.

There is a richness in the Christmas stories beyond the beauty of our nativity scenes. Let's delve deeper into the artistry of Luke and grasp his message—the message of Gabriel in today's Gospel: God has intervened in human history, and God's promises are fulfilled in Jesus.

Today's Action
Take time to study the background to Luke's infancy stories.

Prayer
God who sends messengers of Good News, may we be attentive to what you want us to hear. May we learn to listen in unexpected places and be open to the fulfillment of your promises. Amen.

· · · | · · ·

December 21

St. Maria Faustina Kowalska: Celebrating God's Mercy and Love

Song of Songs 2:8–14 or Zephaniah 3:14–18;
Psalm 33:2–3, 1–12, 20–21; Luke 1:39–35

The Bible is full of great love stories and love songs. Some celebrate human love, like the Song of Songs, and invite us to see there the love God has for us. Others, like today's alternate reading from the Prophet Zephaniah, celebrates God's embrace of "Daughter Jerusalem," who is restored by God's love.

Maria Faustina Kowalska shared with the world her deep love for Jesus and her mystical experiences. These became popularized by Pope John Paul II, her Polish countryman, in the devotion to God's "Divine Mercy."

Faustina was born in 1905, in Polish territory that was part of Germany prior to World War I. She joined the Congregation of the Sisters of Our Lady of Mercy in 1925, where she lived and served humbly. Her private revelations from the Lord emphasized Christ's longing to forgive and are summed up in the image associated with the Divine Mercy devotion.

During a visit to the Sanctuary of Divine Mercy near Krakow in 1997, John Paul II testified that the message of divine mercy sustained him during World War II and in his papacy.

May we experience Christ's love and mercy during the coming Christmas season.

Today's Action
Take part in your parish's communal penance service in these Advent days.

Prayer
God of love, your divine mercy desires to unite us ever more closely to you in your Son, Jesus. As he loved us even to death on the cross, may that same love sustain us all the days of our lives. Amen.

· · · | · · ·

December 22

Hannah and Mary: Joined by a Common Song

1 Samuel 1:24–28; 1 Samuel 2:1, 4–5, 6–7, 8abcd; Luke 1:46–56

St. Luke's infancy stories are like a "bridge" joining Old and New Testaments. When Mary visits her cousin Elizabeth, these two parts of the story of salvation meet. John the Baptist, Elizabeth's son, is the end of the Old Testament line of prophets. Jesus, Mary's son, embodies the New Covenant.

As Mary hears her older relative praise God for promises fulfilled—in their babes-in-womb—Mary breaks out into a song. It praises God's wonderful works, recounted in the Hebrew Scriptures and echoed in Hannah's story (today's First Reading) and *her* song (today's Responsorial).

Scholars draw the obvious parallels: Both Mary and Hannah were women who would have received criticism from their Middle Eastern society—Hannah, unable to bear children; Mary, pregnant before her marriage to Joseph was final.

In both stories God is at work. Hannah bears the child who will grow up to be one of Israel's great prophets—Samuel. Elizabeth bears John, who will herald the Messiah; Mary's song acknowledges this great work of salvation.

As Christians, we are bearers of promises fulfilled. What is our song today?

Today's Action
What sentiments of praise for God's work would you include in *your* song?

Prayer
God of our songs, fill us with divine music. May our voices blend with the choirs of angels, preparing to herald the birth of the Messiah. Let it echo in our lives in the days ahead. Amen.

· · · | · · ·

December 23

Elizabeth: A Woman of Past and Future

MALACHI 3:1–4, 23–24: PSALM 25:4–5, 8–9, 10, 14; LUKE 1:57–66

Elizabeth must have had a pretty good press agent. Her story gets three days' worth of exposure in the run-up to Christmas!

The delightful details of her story are irresistible. She is the elderly, childless wife, favored with a surprise pregnancy. She is the costar in a beautiful encounter between two pregnant cousins. And she is the enigmatic mother who gives the name John to her child.

Hidden in the story is Luke's intention to portray Elizabeth and her husband, Zechariah, in an important symbolic role. Behind them, like hidden images beneath the strokes of a painted masterpiece, are the Old Testament portraits of Abraham and Sarah, and the parents of the prophet Samuel, Elkanah and Hannah.

Elizabeth's age and barrenness echo the stories of those two ancient ancestors of Israel. And in today's Gospel, her joy over the birth of John the Baptist parallels the joy of Sarah in Genesis, at the birth of Isaac.

But Elizabeth also looks forward to the story of the adult Jesus. During Mary's visit, she cries out, "Blessed is she who trusted that the Lord's words to her would be fulfilled." In Luke 8:21 Jesus uses similar words honoring his mother—and all true disciples—as one who hears the word of God and acts upon it.

Today's Action
What part of the infancy story might move you to act as Jesus' disciple today?

Prayer
God of our past and of our future, enrich us with the tradition of faith into which we are born through baptism. Point us to our present and to our future, where we are called to be faithful disciples of your Son. Amen.

December 24

St. Francis of Assisi: Recreating Bethlehem

2 Samuel 7:1–5, 8–11, 16; Psalm 89:2–3, 4–5, 27, 29; Luke 1:67–79

A fond childhood memory for me is setting up my grandmother's huge nativity set, with dozens of figures, depicting various crafts and artisans. When I finished, I liked to put my face close to the figures and imagine being in the scene myself.

Little did I know I was acting out an impulse of the saint who would also be my spiritual father later in life—St. Francis of Assisi.

Every Franciscan's heart is somehow linked to the nativity scene, in part because Francis recreated "a new Bethlehem" near the Italian hilltop village of Greccio in 1223, in a "living nativity."

But a deeper connection for Franciscans is the truth of God-become-human. Francis understood the great act of love in the "attitude of Christ Jesus" who did not cling to divinity but emptied himself and took on our humanity (see Philippians 2:5–11).

Francis strove to imitate this emptying in all he did. He left his prosperous life in Assisi and descended to the marshes to serve the lepers. His words and deeds sought to embody the image of Christ, even to bearing the wounds of his Savior.

On the eve of Christmas, one does not have to be a Franciscan in fact. In the spirit of the poor man of Assisi, we are all invited to step into the nativity scene ourselves!

Today's Action
Spend a few quiet moments near the nativity scene in your church or home and ponder God-become-human.

Prayer
God born into our world, may we stand in awe before the wondrous scene of your Advent. May this holy night awaken in us new faith in the truth of Emmanuel, God-with-us. Amen.

· · · | · · ·

December 25

Christmas Day

Communion Call

Stand in the winter's cold
Where the warmth of animals surrounds the mother's
love,
And distant calls of shepherds,
Fresh from angels' songs
Echo ancient stories of promise.

Unseen observer,
You are circled by centuries of saints,
Companion to martyrs on Rome's bloody sands,
Wise teachers who shaped eloquent creeds,
Kings, queens, commoners, hermits, preachers,
Brave women who crossed seas,
Popes, too—shy now in the encircling darkness.

Beyond them in the shadows
Stand nomads with leathered faces full of fidelity,
The brooding prophets satisfied and smiling,
And the sinner-king, robed in ancestral pride.

They all come home tonight
And take one deep, ageless breath
As the great story's relentless pace
Pauses
In the pinpoint moment
Of God born into our world.

• • • | • • •
Table of Saints and Feast Days

Adolph Kolping (December 4)

Angela Merici (January 27)

Athanasius (May 2)

Elijah

Elizabeth (Feast of the Visitation, May 31)

Elizabeth Ann Seton (January 4)

Frances Xavier Cabrini (November 13)

Francis of Assisi (October 4)

Francis Xavier (December 3)

Frederic Ozanam (September 7)

Gabriel (September 29)

Hannah and Mary

Isaiah

John of the Cross (December 14)

John the Baptist (June 24, August 29)

John XXIII (October 11)

Joseph (March 19, May 1)

Josephine Bakhita (February 8)

Juan Diego (December 9)

Katharine Drexel (March 3)

King David

Lucy (December 13)

Mary (January 1)

Maria Faustina Kowalska (October 5)

Monica (August 27)

Nicholas (December 6)

Our Lady of Guadalupe (December 12)

Peter (June 2, 29)

Ruth

Vincent de Paul (September 27)

Zechariah